HEARTEND

_hydrus

Published by: Hydrus
Photography by: Hydrus
Proofreading by: Gabrielle G.
Cover Design by: Cleo Moran - Devoted Pages Designs
Formatting by: Cleo Moran - Devoted Pages Designs
https://www.devotedpages.com

Manufactured in the United States of America

ISBN: 978-1-7357824-4-7

HAILEY

EMPTY
ALL I DO IS JUST
BLEED ♥

I love, so I accept that I will be hurt.

_hydrus

Dedicated to those of us who hurt.

HeartEND is about how we experience love and some of the journeys we embark on when love strikes our heart.

It's about the numerous complex phases and ever changing stages of the purest human emotions.

It might be a first kiss, a new romance, a guilty pleasure or a sense of loss but love always helps us reach the heavens or crash down upon its shores.

Love gives even when it takes, it heals and embeds its mark and sculpts us into who we are.

"We all open our hearts and in the end this is the love we bleed."
_hydrus

Attraction

There is a magic that brings me to you
and makes me want to never let go
and recover from this spell

_hydrus

An elusive breeze
That steals the sun
A warm romantic
Hiding from one

Escaping passion
Evading claim
Teasing capture
To play the game

Hearts are open
Compassion waits
Pure emotions
Destined our fate

Wanting pleasure
A seductive quest
Living for this moment
That was the test

Proven
_hydrus

I could not imagine
A time quite like this
Desire so deep
Serenity in bliss

A never ending morning
Where the sun heats the skin
Awakening in your arms
Kissing as we grin

Peace in an embrace
Laughter as we cry
Our worlds beyond space
Bonds that will never die

Meant
_hydrus

Wants that blinded
Ignites inside
Grabs the soul
I cannot hide

Eats at my dreams
All fears overcome
My new horizon
We are now one

Together
_hydrus

My pulse races
As the time grows close
All senses tense
You are my host

Vivid the scene
An alluring sight
Our chance seared
Fervid with delight

How many ways
Can you tempt desire
When all lust burns
All ablaze with fire

Provoked intentions
Intense the flame
Inner kindled heat
I will not tame

Fuel
_hydrus

You are a reccurring sunrise that never wanes

Bitten by your beauty
Enchanted kisses nipped
Poison the seduction
Stricken by your lips

Tasting the exotic
Captive and secure
Infectious the attraction
Victim to your cure

Baited
_hydrus

Open eyes
Dream in her wake
Entire thoughts
Cannot escape

Her every breath
Reminds the mind
This walking angel
Is truly mine

An inner strength
Authentic soul
A pure beauty
She makes me whole

I live for us
A perfect peace
Without this love
My life would cease

Everything
_hydrus

Innocence that glared
In a heated stream
Natural purity
A beauty queen

Stellar stance
A pose to draw
Boundless power
Strength to awe

She amazed
In simple whites
Yet in darkness
Owned the night

All desire
Grew with each stare
Sculpted moment
Abstract affair

Catwalk
_hydrus

I sit and pray
That we align
Your nomadic ways
Will be mine

And on that day
When we reach the moon
Life will begin
And I can mend your
wounds

Await
_hydrus

Mesmerized by just her silhouette
Every surface I must inspect

Wondrous lines that evade the stars
Shimmering skin that conceals her scars

Eyes that flutter glistening with tears
In my arms we will fight those fears

I will wait until the endless dawn
Make her mine until we are one

Safe
_hydrus

A burning rose
Amongst heated flames
Watching you
In a springtime rain

All meaning learned
It comes to life
Every time
You arrive

Presence
_hydrus

Connection

Without you I am incomplete
a lost vessel searching for what makes them
whole

_hydrus

In darkness you held my hand
As I fell upon the sands

Lifted me through all the grief
A battered sail stolen by thieves

Rains now poured you washed away
Any pain that slaved my days

Even falling in all defeat
You shared your faith and brought me peace

Gentle words whispered to ease
Lasting calm in a drowning sea

Anchor
_hydrus

Quiet gaze
Thrown my way
Lifted walls
Set me astray

How I yearn
To taste this pill
It tempts from far
Rejects my will

On this day
I chased my fear
Told their soul
They are mine to steal

Crush
_hydrus

So many choices
When only you matter

Obvious
_hydrus

You were my beginning
When my ending was clear
Unmasked my dread
And extinguished my tears

I found in you
An awakening gust
A lifelong dance
Its song built on trust

Sweet discovery
Infinite in truth
Beautifully conceived
Divine in its youth

A connecting spirit
Transcending through time
My beloved companion
Universally mine

Dawn
_hydrus

You are an angel

in a sky full of storms

_hydrus

Single the touch
Making hairs stand
Light up my heart
Taking their man

Power
_hydrus

You are the up to my down
An alpha to my omega
My heartfelt song
That feels every note

A vast ocean full of dreams
Nestled in every smile
An everlasting reach
Grabbing hold of my soul

Treasured
_hydrus

Black room
Provides my shield
In its echoes
Shapes are revealed

Nights blanket
Brings you to me
Bound in flesh
Sweet harmony

We slowly dance
Caress to feel
Divine existence
The trance concealed

Yet light appears
You slip away
A faint discovery
Brings me decay

Vision
_hydrus

You will always be the alpha to my zeta

_hydrus

Leaves
Sway in the trees
As the gentle grasses
Grow
In the breeze
Sunlight flickers
Through each and every stem
An overwhelming happiness
Bundles
My heaven

Connection
_hydrus

You were my every answer
To questions never asked
An unknown adventure
Shadowed by our pasts

Giving me direction
A compass for my will
Forgiveness and affection
Loving was your skill

A complicated map
You paved to see the way
Even if distressed
Life lived was everyday

Always at my side
So tenderly complete
Words cannot reflect
How much you mean to me

Beacon
_hydrus

Romance

Ones path through life can fully be measured
through the eyes of the one they consider true

_hydrus

You held my hand
As I fell in space
A simple plan
It became my base

Never once
Did your grip retire
You grabbed me firm
Even in fire

That sweet touch
Carries on in us
Always reaching
Divine the trust

Forever catching
Those unwanted drops
Longing living
Engulfed in love

Holden
_hydrus

The second I froze
Gave into her eyes
A stunning beauty
Luck so surmised

Frantic the thoughts
Eager my fear
Anxious the beat
Of my lover so near

Melting my senses
I became disarrayed
Perfection on earth
Emboldened to play

Wanting their all
Consumed by a kiss
Eternal my love
A match made for this

Fate
_hydrus

All I wish
Is your life with mine
Your small caresses
Us intertwined

The moon and stars
Aligned to show
You are the one
All I know

All
_hydrus

The morning sun
Shines on your face
I hold your hand
Fingers interlace

There is no place
I would rather be
Than in your arms
Eternally

True
_hydrus

You are worth every thorn and every scratch...
I only bleed for you

_hydrus

At glance I see
Peering back at me
Skin that is pleased
As kisses tease

Upon my flesh
Is inked your stamp
A lasting mark
Where teeth had clamped

Yours
_hydrus

My everlasting
Winter breeze
Springtime rainfall
Summer ease

A blue horizon
Tides so free
Birthed from the clouds
From heavens tree

Lips so tender
Full of rainbow hues
Longing eyes
And I love yous

A living dream
Where shadows hide
Never to wake
Without her side

Eve
_hydrus

The heavens breathe every time we kiss

An instance
Does not pass
In which my thoughts
Can only bask

Every season
For every time
The love we felt
Became enshrined

We
_hydrus

I found heaven
It stumbles and falls
Full of regrets
Filled with faults

I found heaven
With questions to all
Insecure moments
Silent withdrawals

I found heaven
All dressed in black
Hidden in darkness
Mourning each crack

I found heaven
Bathed in all fear
Doubting herself
Scolding her tears

I found heaven
She might not agree
All I see is perfection
I want her all for me

Flawless
_hydrus

Sensual

I found a relentless hunger for your passion
and crave to be your meal

Her skin tender
Lightly iced
In my arms
Warmth ignites

Soft kisses
And bitten lips
Tasting tongues
With fingertips

Pounding hearts
Tracing lines
Indulging movements
Bodies grind

Tingling feelings
Breathless air
This forever
No compare

Endless
_hydrus

Bathed in your scent
I quickly seduce
Open you wide
Quench on your juice

Hands buried in flesh
Tongues trace every line
Consumed in our passion
In your taste I must dine

Greeting
_hydrus

Coiled is the serpent
Awaiting its prey
Hiding its prize
Curled in display

Fangs at the ready
Poisoned to please
Oozing in venom
Seducing with ease

Impatiently waiting
Hardened to strike
Injecting its liquids
Yet swallowed in spite

Bitten
_hydrus

Sitting in darkness
I stare at the flicker
Of a wanted moan
A thirst grows thicker

Melting hot wax
Slowly drips to unveil
A hardened thick shaft
You kneel without fail

Gripping my skin
As you lick to oblige
Our trance reconnects
I look in your eyes

Take what is yours
Devour me whole
I am yours to command
You are mine to control

One
_hydrus

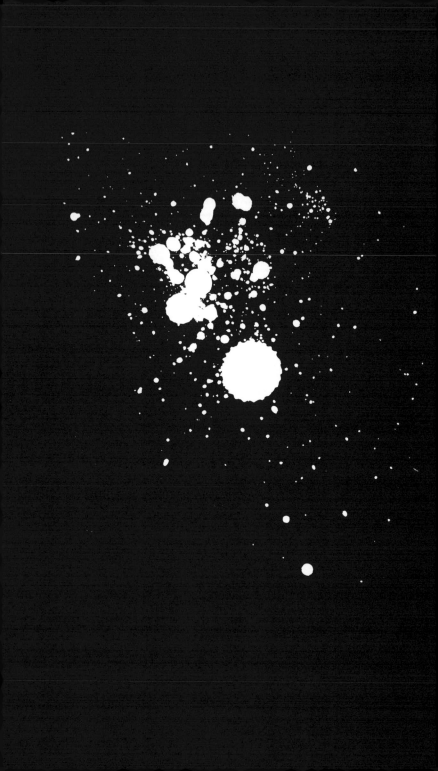

In your shell
I want to live
Dive inside
Thrust and give

Drink your ocean
Eat the moon
Bathe in waves
Have you consumed

Hunger
_hydrus

Threaded limbs
Enter every curve
Soft embraces
Waken every nerve

Sleep still lingers
Anxious hands explore
Dormant flesh
Waiting for some more

Sliding kisses
Move to take their mark
Entering spaces
To ignite a spark

Once they meet
Gentle licks will glide
Tasting heat
So deep inside

Yearning
_hydrus

Luscious Lips
Dripping red
Drenching tip
Painted head

Licking shaft
Throbbing veins
Every muscle
Gently played

Bodies bend
Stroking skin
Whispered groans
Sensual grins

Open throat
Takes me in
Ingested moans
Morning sin

Sunrise
_hydrus

Hidden eyes
Spying forms
Pleasured beats
Bounded norms

Masters rules
Obeying hands
Lucid grips
Spanked commands

Restrained hunger
Arousing scent
Judges sentence
No repent

Knotted wrists
Leathers worn
Open mouths
Clothes are torn

Hands and knees
A prepped display
Behaved attraction
Ready to play

Waiting
_hydrus

I want to explore every inch and even more

_hydrus

Fingerprints
Adorn my thighs
Where her hands
Found their prize

Inner walls
Lapped to ease
Arching backs
As lovers please

Intertwined
Bodies twist
Drenched in oils
Lips are kissed

Tongues explore
Inside we dive
Soaked in lust
Feeling so alive

Encounter
_hydrus

Darkened room
Engulfs my night
Hidden hands
Searching in spite

An eager want
As I wait to feel
Probing fingers
Trying to unseal

Starving cravings
The erotic needs
Savage longing
That divulge my greed

Swollen hardness
Twitching in place
Painting you
Leaving my trace

Marked
_hydrus

Obsession

I only live for every moment with you
and even that is not enough

_hydrus

Sweat covers
Every inch
Muscles tense
Nerves flinch

Isolated
Thoughts loom
Assuming life
Within their tomb

Consumed emotions
Time is still
Daytime dreams
Yearning thrills

Will I see
Who I adore
Or will this chase
End once more

Surveil
_hydrus

How can his hands
Be touching what's mine
Marking the surface
Taking their time

Mending hearts broken
Healing the wounds
Understanding misfortune
Unwittingly doomed

Groom
_hydrus

Left are the scars
That drape deep inside
Remind me of us
And the things we both hide

Elaborately tailored
They hang off our skin
Abrasively clever
Adorned as we sinned

Anger and conflict
Taint our own flesh
Searching for silence
We venture in jest

Hunting for someone
To please and proclaim
Taking our bodies
As trophies of shame

Suitors
_hydrus

Manic concerns
Cutting lines
Burned bulbs
Sculpted rhymes

Odd encounters
Hinted thrills
Surprised laughter
Uneasy chills

One mistake
Lush in drink
Followed by
Him I think

Decisions
_hydrus

I hope my scent still

drips from your hands
_hydrus

Does she taste your lips
And ride your pains away
Or whisper dirty secrets
When you are tied to play

Other
_hydrus

Veiled accomplice
Devious fates
Bending rules
To take my mate

So unwise
Playing this game
A poisoned prize
With unclean fame

Rendezvous
Sleazy rooms
Scented candles
Odors loom

Silent calls
Evading eyes
Different stories
So many lies

Unknown facts
All is known
I will wait
When you are alone

Knowing
_hydrus

I left you
But you took
My Soul

_hydrus

Open madness
Distant sleep
Ticking time
Voices creep

In my head
Chaos plays
Prisoned bed
I lay awake

Taunting dreams
Of escapades
Secret schemes
Nightly raids

Will this end
Or ever cease
No return
I will not sleep

Counting
_hydrus

Let me drown
Breathe no more
I cannot be
Upon this shore

As I fall
You will see
All the beauty
That could not be

Alone
_hydrus

Temptation

The thirst to drink what I cannot drink
is hypnotically intoxicating

_hydrus

Voices sneak
Into my mind
Wanting savoring
Forbidden wine

My only ask
Is a simple sip
Taste the odor
Lick the tip

Drops of pleasure
Fill my void
Tempted treasure
Quenched destroyed

Now the vines
Make their nest
Seductive spirits
Contently jest

For their odor
And toxic scent
Addictive brew
From which I repent

Expired
_hydrus

Naked sins
Wrapped in spells
Dim lit rooms
In dark motels

Parking lots
A hidden maze
Any place
To feed this slave

Opportunity
_hydrus

Eyes disguised
A painted feast
Drawing lips
Hiding deceit

Shaded veils
Deceptions rise
Whispered words
Conceal reprise

A tested dance
For this new song
Witnessed cheat
All things gone wrong

Yet this event
Seduced to stay
The captured corpse
Cannot get away

Saga
_hydrus

Demons linger
Ravens fly
In their wings
I hear them cry

Wanting souls
Wanting flings
These are tastes
For unholy things

Murdered
_hydrus

We will be

rewritten for our mistakes
_hydrus

Why must I lay
In my blood
Watching breaths
White winged doves

Cloudy nights
Torrid pains
Dimming lights
Cold remains

Sultry dish
Carved to course
Slashing lives
No remorse

Now I wait
Puddles drown
Bonded fate
Upside down

Sedated
_hydrus

In her slumber
I tease her thoughts
Insert my visions
Indulge her fog

Infect her dreams
With newer tales
Answer lies
Hide my scales

For morning brings
An awakened boast
Enlightened signs
Rumors from ghost

An untested dawn
Erased to start
A false reality
We will never part

Pretenders
_hydrus

In our past
We crossed lives
Familiar feelings
Now disguised

New situations
Norms to deal
Emotions linger
They still are real

Lives at play
As we evade
Tortured days
Nights will fade

Yet again
When paths are crossed
Reality hits
Of the us we lost

Still
_hydrus

A heated moment
Spoken truths
Opened scars
That lead me to you

Spark
_hydrus

A subtle brush
Winks and stare
Little jesters
All unaware

Hinted crush
A stolen smile
Heartbeats rush
So infantile

Guided lessons
Planned attire
Dark exchanges
Both retire

In this hunt
Skin will mix
Prepped desires
With new tricks

Fling
_hydrus

Conceived denial
This has brought
To my chest
When all is fought

A continued mess
Repeated flare
Always distressed
Without any care

Words are many
Then are few
Abstraction sets
Lifeless clues

Now the opening
Swells to claim
Hanging bait
Placing blame

At this time
The seas retreat
Leaving options
At our feet

New excursions
Search to taste
Obstructing truth
Just to replace

Overboard
_hydrus

Betrayal

My ignorance never could have imagined
that your final act would be so final

_hydrus

Drink the juices
Take the pain
Enjoy the moment
While it reigned

Fall the tears
Crave the look
Awoke the instant
As you took

Quick the sample
Long the stride
Lives the story
Of when we died

Past
_hydrus

Betrayed in life
Resentful hate
A tempted skin
Taken in haste

Mounted steed
Pleasures hide
Confessed in hope
Yet not denied

Ridden
_hydrus

Alone you stand
In a strangers hands

Silently you plea
To only be with me

Yet there you are
Falling way too far

Your new destiny
Plagued in sad agony

The Moment
_hydrus

Sinister lies
You pretend to play
Abducted all senses
Obstructed the way

Created a path
Adorned with my soul
Blessed by desire
Intended to troll

Simple ways born
Made not escape
The trance was naive
Pain made to be great

Run to then climb
A limitless gait
Realities victims
Perished by fate

Fall
_hydrus

I will paint the world with your ashes

_hydrus

Tears rain and plague the skies
Saddened notions of a oath that died
Although feelings did not grasp this fate
When legs opened and engulfed his state

Flesh pushed knowing of its course
Now one cowers to feel remorse
Cravings happen and are quenched with ease
Until the victim pleads again to please

Offender
_hydrus

I pray you gazed
Into his face
Screamed and moaned
In your disgrace

Knowing a sadness
Perched upon his throne
Hungry in madness
To be disowned

Reenacting a role
Pretending to bleed
Happily undressed
The hypocritical steed

Yet the mount was made
Pleasures were brief
Begin all your days
Reliving this grief

Illusionist
_hydrus

In times like these
One slowly weeps
Nights are long
There is no sleep

All one knows
As they lay
We will live on
And still decay

Confessed
_hydrus

Subtle spheres
Appear in the sky
In my illusions
I slowly die

As I slept
One took the bait
Laid my soul
Ate my mate

Tears then came
I lay still
Nocturnal creature
Took her will

A wanted fight
To kill by name
Until the hunted
Was in the game

Unknown to me
The two had danced
There was no slumber
In my romance

Now they feast
On their deceit
I still search
For love to meet

Mislead
_hydrus

Written words
Playfully please
Meant to forget
Put you at ease

Yet I remember
Letters cannot erase
The moment you swallowed
Embraced your disgrace

You chose to be taken
Erected in vain
I was mistaken
Live with this stain

Wronged
_hydrus

I hope you enjoyed the ride
Hollow emptiness filling you
Hopefully you survive
To relive every moment you were
Untrue

Thirsty
_hydrus

Loss

A part of my past will never be revived
the moment you were no more

_hydrus

The day forgotten
Not by choice
Avoided thoughts
A distant voice

Of what we were
Moments past
Lives reborn
Yet could not last

Emotions wane
Cannot pretend
Clouded days
I lost my friend

Unrest
_hydrus

Blame I feel
For this waste
A bitter end
Such lifeless haste

I chose a path
And ended dead
With no escape
My new found dread

A bumbling fool
Unwilling host
Inside myself
An angered ghost

Beyond I watch
Mourning in wait
Forever sleep
Haunting my mate

Shadow
_hydrus

Crushed was the earth
No more cares
All alone
Nothing compares

My loving beat
Had ceased to be
Away forever
This cannot be

Begging the gods
To strike me down
I lost my love
Was never found

Over
_hydrus

You left without a trace
Abandoned
I waited
And wait
Words and feelings
Erased from the earth
Only etched in my heart
A wound I must carry
Yet every moment I still cherish
A fool for loving you

Pain
_hydrus

I found myself buried in what was never love

_hydrus

Fallen ashes
A fear foreseen
Scared resistance
Endless screams

My runaway
Illusions ghost
Just disappeared
From her host

Sweet misery
Won this game
Broken answers
Constant pain

New suspicions
Will never find
Darkened visions
Erased from time

Run
_hydrus

Showers fall
Drench the ground
Grey stones thrown
Adorn their mounds

Shallow puddles
Paint the leaves
Dewy webs
Dressed to grieve

Silent fog
Clears in light
Kneeling gestures
Tranquil sights

Quiet moments
As we depart
Droplets find
Their resting heart

Poured
_hydrus

Withered romance
A destined fade
An empty silence
Made to betray

Words without meaning
A deafening tone
Absent the feeling
Of a love once owned

Where did we languish
How did we die
When all was woven
Yet built on lies

Still no regrets
Or maliced needs
My sadness bests
On us it feeds

Rest
_hydrus

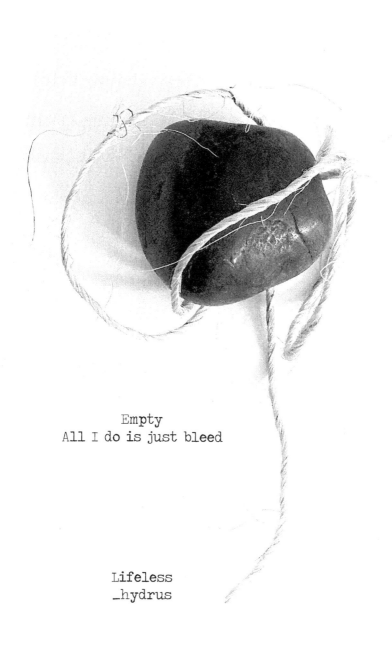

Empty
All I do is just bleed

Lifeless
_hydrus

To have you in my heart
Was a gift unknown
Until it was taken
I stood alone
Only the pain
Found the will to survive
Reminding me
Of love
That simply
Just died

Gone
_hydrus

Etched engraved
Every line you marked
A heavenly perfection
Inked on my heart

Every kiss you placed
All the gestures embarked
The smiles you made
Faded with your spark

Dark
_hydrus

Waves wash away
Saddened footsteps in sand
Gone to a place
One cannot understand

Vanished this love
Taken from my grips
Now it drowns
Bloodied hands still resist

Worthless my life
Without this I cease
Emptiness grows
Darkness now feasts

I too want to swim
And fade into the sea
Hopelessly searching
For the one meant for me

Sundown
_hydrus

The heart remembers
When it was caught
Grabbed from the air
When it was lost

An etched memory
Never in grey
Only to grow
Strong and unscathed

Relentless the beat
Aware of its pulse
Pounding together
Love with no cost

Blessed with forever
Even when it leaves
Giving us life
As the blood grieves

Always
_hydrus

Healing

I am dressed in countless wounds
only to be mended by your love

_hydrus

You inspired me to grow
Be an everlasting snow
Blanketing the earth
Expressing all I know

Fearless to the wind
Gracious to the sky
Kind to all the stars
Wherever they may lie

Live amongst the stream
Fly with the crows
Be the better man
Who loves all he knows

Lessons
_hydrus

Rains wilt
Turning grey
Fallen thorns
Bend and frey

Slowly rise
With the open sky
Receiving grace
From weeping eyes

Finding faith
In a barren sea
Life recovered
On bloodied knees

Wake
_hydrus

Erased are the wounds
Yet the pain still lives
The haunting loss
That does not forgive

You went away
I will not retreat
A never ending mark
That will never leave

Today we weep
All day I dread
Tomorrow we will see
My life has fled

Remain
_hydrus

All is forgotten
Yet the heart still mourns
The shredded path
That our troubles tore

Love canceled
A rebooted birth
Separate ways
I learned my worth

New
_hydrus

I followed you in Life and I will live for you in soul

_hydrus

My wings were broken
I was to blame
A selfish heartbreak
I caused the pain

Foolish heartache
Caused by the fool
Naive the idiot
Abandoned rules

Life learned
My will was torched
Failures burn
Regrets were forged

Discovery
_hydrus

From these branches
Came the fall
The love we shared
As autumn called

Our spring went dry
Yet leaves remained
Our love still stands
Until the rains

Poured
_hydrus

Trials heal
When they do not kill
Leave you barren
As your ink spills

Words become empty
Yet the light still fights
That unforgiving hurt
Your departure will ignite

Released
_hydrus

You took me to the depths of myself and there I found your love

_hydrus

We were a story
A never ending past
A former version
With an afflicted cast

But time corrected
Made feelings change
New endings rewritten
Ever afters explained

A new found beginning
Where love was reclaimed
The voices were silenced
And our timeless remained

Chapter
_hydrus

∞

And in the end
I felt the pain
Of lost romances
Where hurt was gained

It made me whole
A newer man
It took its toll
I understand

Yet scars and tears
Wounded ways
Some lonely years
Desperate days

Lead me to this
My new found place
The older me
I had replaced

Invisible spirits
Watching over me
Awakened my senses
And helped me just be

There was a light
In my darkened soul
Where I felt you once
When I was whole

HeartEND
_hydrus

I live for you

Thank You

C./G.

"Do you believe in destiny? That even the powers of time can be altered for a single purpose? That the luckiest man who walks on this earth is the one who finds… true love?"

Bram Stoker, Dracula

Also by _hydrus

ENDVISIBLE

A collection of poems about the endless feeling of being invisible while going
through the emotions and sometimes cruelties of life. Illustrated by the
author's own photography, this book guides us through grief, loss and love in a dark
and inspiring way typical to how Hydrus's writing helps us cope with reality.

AWAKEND

Tarots cards, much like poems, have the ability to paint a vivid picture of what
once was or what could be. They delve into the subtleties that we all carry within
ourselves and the secrets that make us who we are. AwakEND is an immersion
into the world of tarot and its mysteries. Read it one way, then another, and let
the words guide you into the meaning of each card. Allow chance and curiosity to
accompany you on this incredible journey and let your heart awaken to hope even
after having thought everything was lost... And who knows what secrets you might
find out about yourself...

DARKEND

Is a small look into the world I call my reality. Through poems, photography and
art, I try to capture the ups and downs of this voyage we call life, and sometimes
I refer to it as just existing. Embedded in my words are stories of emotions and
feelings that range from the darkest of moments to times of having some type
of hope for resolve. Life is raw and ever-evolving, and we always seem to put
ourselves last overall. Time proves to be quite relentless. I hope that we all find
common ground through our everyday struggles and in the end, understand that
love, although painful at times, can provide so many answers.

So the question then becomes *"how can we better love ourselves?"*

About The Author

Anonymous poet, photographer and artist,
Hydrus documents through his poems the darkness and the
glimmers of life taunting us when we are in the shadows, as
well as many of the little things which make a
colossal impact on who we are.

Connect with hydrus:

Website: www.hydruspoetry.com
Instagram: instagram.com/hydruspoetry
Facebook: https://www.facebook.com/hydruspoetry

Write your Soul

_hydrus

Made in United States
Orlando, FL
29 April 2022

17333199R00078